D0945939

The Wonder Series

Sea OTTER River OTTER

Written by

SANDRA CHISHOLM ROBINSON

Illustrated by

GAIL KOHLER OPSAHL

and

MARJORIE C. LEGGITT

Denver Museum of Natural History
and Roberts Rinehart Publishers

Other books in The Wonder Series include
  The Wonder of Wolves
  Mountain Lion: Puma, Panther, Painter, Cougar
  Eagles: Hunters of the Sky
  The Everywhere Bear
  Bats: Swift Shadows in the Twilight

Text copyright © 1993 Sandra Chisholm Robinson

Artwork copyright © 1993 Denver Museum of
  Natural History

All rights reserved

Published in the United States of America by
  Roberts Rinehart Publishers
  Post Office Box 666
  Niwot, Colorado 80544

Published in Great Britain, Ireland, and Europe by
  Roberts Rinehart Publishers
  Main Street, Schull, West Cork
  Republic of Ireland

Published in Canada by
  Key Porter Books
  70 The Esplanade
  Toronto, Ontario M5E 1R2

Library of Congress Catalog Card Number
  93-084962

International Standard Book Number
  1-879373-41-6

Manufactured in the United States of America.

Author's Acknowledgments

Sea Otter River Otter is the fourth book that I have written in the Wonder Series and the fourth opportunity to work with designer and artist Gail Kohler Opsahl. Gail approaches the many challenges that come with doing books like this with, "Let me think about it . . . I know we can do it . . . I got it!" Gail, thank you. Also, thanks to Jane Griess for her knowledge and the use of her many resources on river otters. A special note of appreciation goes to the reviewers from Great Smoky Mountains National Park, Friends of the Sea Otter, and the Monterey Bay Aquarium. George Robinson was very helpful in contributing to the "Tiddly Frogs" game. And I want to give special thanks to my son, Garrett, who keeps things in perspective by reminding me that—like otters—it's important for parents and kids to take time to play!

A poster, *The Otter Alphabet*, accompanies this book. For copies ($5.00 per poster plus $2.50 per order for shipping and handling) call Roberts Rinehart Publishers, 1-800-352-1985.

Sea OTTER River OTTER

Contents

Thayer

OTTERS A TO Z

Lately I have been doing a lot of traveling and working on airplanes. In fact, several sections of this book were written at 30,000 feet. Sometimes, if you can't sleep or you forgot to bring a good book to read, a plane flight can seem very long. Quite often after looking over my shoulder for a minute or two, people sitting on either side of me would ask, "What are you doing?"

When I told them I was writing a book, they always said, "Really! What's it about?"

"Otters . . . the book is about river and sea otters," I said.

Their reactions were amazingly similar. They would immediately smile as if they were remembering something pleasant and they would say, "You know, I love otters." Often they would tell me stories about otters they had seen in zoos or in the wild.

A woman from Alaska who lived in a cabin on an isolated lake told me that even at a distance she could always tell the difference between beavers and otters. "Always busy with chores, beavers swim in straight lines," she said. "But when otters cross the lake, they dive and roll and chase each other. They always look as if they are thoroughly enjoying themselves."

Perhaps people smile when they think of otters because many otter traits—playfulness, curiosity, and sociability—remind us of the best in ourselves.

Indeed, otters provide opportunities for us to celebrate our accomplishments in reversing some of the negative impacts we have had on our environment. Otters have recently been successfully reintroduced into areas where they had been wiped out by excessive hunting, pollution, or habitat destruction.

———————

Artist Marjorie Leggitt had a lot of fun drawing an otter alphabet. As you look through the book, be sure to find all twenty-six letters.

From A to Z, we hope that whether you are reading the stories, following a maze, playing "Tiddly Frogs," or being an "otter editor," you will thoroughly enjoy yourself. Because the book—like the animal—is a celebration of play!

ABALONE
a marine snail, is
a favorite food of
sea otters.

Otter Hunt

"Tap, tap, tap." The boy groaned as he rolled over on his back in the sand. "Tap, tap, tap." He smiled in his sleep. His mother was tapping her large stirring spoon against the edge of the heavy cooking kettle. The smell of simmering beef stew seasoned with herbs from her garden made his stomach rumble.

"Ouch!" The boy's eyes popped open as he slapped a fly biting his arm. He sat up abruptly and was blinded by bright sunlight reflected from cresting waves.

He sucked in his breath sharply. He was not in his mother's neat clapboard house in Boston. He was on the coast of a place called California. He leaped to his feet and ran to the water's edge. Tobias shaded his eyes as he searched for the white sails of his uncle's ship. But the blue expanse of water stretched without interruption to the horizon.

Tobias's uncle, Captain Thornton, sailed from Boston along the northwestern coast of the United States. He carried goods to trade with the Indians for furs, primarily sea otter furs. The captain then sailed to China with the thick, chocolate colored furs that were described as "the richest and the most delicious fur in the world." There he traded the pelts for spices and other luxuries that Bostonians desired.

Captain Thornton and Tobias's father were brothers. But Tobias hardly remembered his father; he died at sea when Tobias was a small boy. Captain Thornton, who had no children, assumed responsibility for Tobias. Tobias knew that his mother and Captain Thornton did not always agree on how Tobias should be raised. His mother had lost the most recent argument, and so Tobias was on his first voyage.

"Tap, tap, tap." There was that sound again. Tobias felt a surge of hope. Maybe people were camped on the beach—maybe they were his rescuers! He walked in the direction of the sound.

As Tobias picked his way among the rocks of the shoreline he studied the cliffs that in some places plunged into the sea. In spite of the sun's warmth, he shivered. In his whole life he had never felt so abandoned and alone—except when he said good-bye to his mother at the dock in Boston.

His mother had pressed a leather bound journal into his hands. Tobias remembered her words, "Every day just before you lose daylight, write to me in this book. I will sit very quietly, and I will listen."

Tobias had said, "But mother, I will be far away. You won't be able to hear me."

Tobias's mother had smiled. "I won't be listening with my ears," she said, "I'll be listening with my heart."

Tobias looked back at his footprints in the wet sand. He had walked a long way. But the tapping sound was now close. Cautious, he approached a group of large rocks and crouched behind them. Very slowly, he lifted his head and peered over them.

In spite of his disappointment in not finding people, he grinned. There in a sheltered cove was a large group of animals floating in the sea. The animals' sleek coats sparkled in the sunlight. Some of the creatures rested on shore and combed their fur with their front claws.

Tobias watched in wonder as the animals, floating on their backs, tapped clams against rocks resting on their chests. When they broke open the shells, they scooped out the soft animals inside. The boy chuckled as one animal, after finishing its meal, carefully licked each paw.

Tobias winced as he watched an animal nip off the spines of a purple, spiky creature. Tobias had once seen a drawing of such an animal in a book. "It must be a sea urchin," he said out loud.

Tobias marveled at how busy the animals were. Some swam close to the shore searching for food among the rocks. Eating the crabs and other small creatures attached to the plant, one animal picked at a large pile of seaweed that it carried on its chest.

Watching the animals feed, Tobias realized how hungry he was. No longer fearing the tapping sound, Tobias stepped from behind the rocks and moved onto the beach of the protected cove. The animals were not frightened by him. Although they carefully watched his movements, they continued to go about their business.

Tobias moved down the beach and followed an animal trail leading into a wooded area. He found a stump that held a small pool of rainwater. He drank thirstily.

The forest was dark and cool—too dark. Tobias felt better in the bright sunlight and he returned to the sheltered cove. As he sat on the sand, he noticed that the animals were finding crabs and other small animals along the shore. The boy followed their example and he, too, searched for food among the rocks.

As Tobias watched the orange glow of the sun over the water, he thought about his mother and his promise to write in his journal. But his journal was back on the ship. How would he keep his promise? He would write to his mother in his thoughts.

Dear Mother: You are probably wondering why I am not on the ship with Captain Thornton. I am afraid the captain is upset with me for what I did. I was only trying to be brave.

As we followed the coast of California, the weather became very bad. I can still remember how my stomach felt as the ship rose and fell with the waves. The ship shuddered and the deck groaned. The rain was falling so hard, it stung our faces.

Captain Thornton searched the shoreline for a sheltered bay where we could anchor and sit out the storm.

Mother, I am ashamed that I felt so afraid. I wanted to be like my father. Captain Thornton told me he had been a brave man.

Captain Thornton, the crew, and the few passengers on deck could see nothing through the driving rain. Captain Thornton yelled above the roar of the wind and sea, "If we could just get a break in the weather—just one look at that coastline."

I looked at the ship's towering mast. I thought that maybe from the top of the mast I could get a better view. I admit, I did not think my plan through very well at all.

I mounted the shrouds and can still feel the pain of the wet ropes cutting into my palms. As I climbed, I heard the captain call to me. But I was already set on my course. The rain blinded me. I raised my hand to wipe my eyes when a blast of wind caught me and threw me into the sea.

The water was so cold I gasped for air. The wooden hull of the ship loomed closer. I gulped water and thought for sure I was dying. I couldn't stop my teeth from chattering. I know it was not just the cold. I was afraid.

Now I, too, rose and fell with the waves. Suddenly something bumped my back. I whirled around and grabbed a barrel that was floating close to me. I watched a chair float by. Unable to help me in any other way, the crew had thrown things into the water that they hoped I would grab onto to help me float.

I grasped the barrel tightly and laid my head down on the rough wood. I was so tired. I must have fallen asleep. The next thing I remember, I was on the beach and dreaming of home.

I miss you, Mother. I know Captain Thornton will rescue me. I will be home soon. I love you and I know you're listening. I don't feel so lonely anymore.

Tobias curled up on the warm sand and fell asleep.

As the days passed, Tobias spent most of his time in the sheltered cove. He had fun watching the sea otters. He observed them until he could tell them apart. Tobias named them from scars, fur color, or their peculiar habits.

Although the otters spent almost all of their time in the water, one otter in particular frequently came on shore. He was a large otter and moved slowly. The fur on his face was very gray. He often came within a few feet of the boy. Tobias named him "Old Man" and had long conversations with him. Tobias, of course, did all of the talking. Sometimes Old Man and Tobias sat quietly—but separately—and watched the other otters play. Although the otters did not seem to fear the boy, they kept their distance.

Tobias was always moved by the mothers and pups. They seemed very much like people in the affection they had for one another. Each mother had only one pup. She lavished it with attention. The pup usually rode on the mother's stomach. Tobias laughed as he watched the younger pups attempt to follow their mothers as they dove for food. Born buoyant, the young pups popped to the surface when they tried to dive. They contented themselves with floating on the surface and sticking their heads under the water so they could watch their mothers.

Tobias named one particular mother "Sad Eyes." He had watched the mother and pup for several days. But one morning he noticed that the pup was not jumping on and off his mother's stomach. The pup lay very still. After watching for a morning, Tobias knew that the pup was dead. However, the mother carried the poor dead pup for three days and even tried to groom and nurse it.

Tobias was always amazed by the antics of the "Robber." This animal made his living by stealing food from other otters. Tobias was shocked at Robber's behavior. Robber watched as a mother, leaving her young on the surface, dove to the bottom for food. Robber grabbed the pup, waited for the mother to surface, and then handed over the pup only after the mother gave up her food.

One night as Tobias "wrote" to his mother in his thoughts, he recalled what Captain Thornton had told him about sea otters.

Dear Mother: As I get to know the sea otters better, I often think about what Captain Thornton told me about them on the ship.

The captain said that sea otters were being hunted out. He said that the beginning of the end for the sea otter started in the mid-1700s. A Danish explorer, Vitus Bering, and his crew were shipwrecked on a desolate island in the north Pacific Ocean. Vitus Bering died, and his crew was left weak and sick. The men lived in deserted foxholes and had only roots and herbs to eat. But the men were saved because sea otters came to shore on the island. The animals were unafraid, and the men killed them easily with clubs. The sea otters provided both food and clothing for the men.

Throughout the winter, the men became greedy and killed many of the animals. The expedition scientist complained to the officers about the slaughter, but nothing was done. In the spring the sailors built a ship and, carrying many otter pelts, sailed from the island. When they reached port, there was much excitement. Now people knew where the otters could be found. Because of the rich market in China, otter fur was very valuable.

In the beginning, otters were hunted by people in kayaks. One hunter paddled while the other clubbed the trusting animals. Over the years, the animals grew wary and were not so easily approached. Then they were hunted with spears. Sometimes nets were spread in the seaweed beds where the otters lived, and when they became tangled in the nets the helpless otters drowned.

Captain Thornton said that before white people became interested in otter fur, the Indians hunted them only sometimes. But as the trade increased, some Indians loaded their kayaks on the big ships and hunted otters for the white captains.

The captain said that groups of native hunters in kayaks surrounded the animals. The hunters slapped the water with their paddles and forced the animals to dive over and over again until they were tired. Then the animals were speared.

Now in some places along the coast, wooden towers are built and the otters are shot with long range guns.

This will likely make you sad, Mother. It is one thing to talk about hunting some animal for its fur. It is quite another thing, once you have gotten to know it. But the furs are beautiful, and people risk their lives to get them.

Well, I must seek shelter for the night. I love you.

Tobias estimated that about thirty animals shared this cove. If Tobias were rescued, this group of otters represented a small fortune for his uncle and the crew. Tobias would be a hero if he shared his secret.

As the days passed, Tobias, like the sea otters, settled into a routine of food gathering. He even figured out how to extract the soft meat from the spiny sea urchin.

And although Tobias was alone, he was surprised that he did not feel lonely. However, watching the mother otters care for their young, Tobias felt a great sadness that he might never see his own mother again.

As his confidence grew, Tobias frequently left the cove and explored the woods and beaches along the coast. One day as he walked the shore, he found himself intently studying a speck of white in the distance. Probably just a gull, he thought. But as he continued to watch, it grew larger and larger. Tobias realized that he was looking at the taut sails of a ship.

Tobias began to jump up and down and wave his arms. He took off his shirt and waved it in the air. Finally, in the calm waters, the ship drew closer. A boat was lowered over the side. Tobias watched as it approached the shore. Captain Thornton stepped out of the boat. Tobias extended his hand, but his uncle grabbed him in a huge bear hug. Tobias's eyes misted over. The captain held him at arm's length. "You're a strong boy, Tobias. I knew you would make it." The captain looked sternly at the boy. "What you did was brave, but foolish, Son."

Tobias kicked the sand with his toe. "I'm sorry, Sir. I wanted to make my father proud. You said he was a brave man."

Captain Thornton looked away and studied the waves for a long time. Finally, he cleared his throat and abruptly said, "Well, we've traded with the Indians for a few otter furs, but it seems we've hunted the poor creatures out. Didn't make as much as we'd hoped, but you'll still see China and then home to Boston."

Tobias thought of his secret in the cove. Those otters were worth a lot of money. They had become so accustomed to him, that a hunter could almost walk right up to them. Captain Thornton and the crew had been good to him. The profits would mean a lot to their families.

Tobias looked in the direction of the sheltered cove and thought of the otters—their shimmery, sleek bodies rolling in the sunlit waters and the mothers tending their pups. He thought of them sleeping on their backs, with their paws over their eyes or resting on their chests. He smiled slightly as he thought of his "talks" with Old Man and the antics of Robber. He thought of Sad Eyes and her devotion to her dead pup.

"Well, Son, the crew can hardly wait to see you," Captain Thornton said and started toward the boat.

Tobias hesitated and looked in the direction of the sheltered cove.

With a puzzled look on his face, the captain turned back. "Are you ready to leave, Tobias?"

Tobias looked back at the cove and at the captain. It was so difficult to choose . . .

THE END?

Every day we are faced with many choices. Sometimes it is easy to choose. You prefer chocolate instead of vanilla ice cream. But everyone faces tough choices. Put yourself in Tobias's place and choose for him. Write your own ending to "Otter Hunt." If you're curious to know how the author ended the story, she has left you a clue in one of the activities in this book.

Happy Hunting (for clues, that is)!

_____

_____

_____

_____

_____

_____

Seafood Buffet

You and your family are on vacation on the California coast. It's dinnertime, everyone is hungry. You pass a restaurant sign that reads: "Seafood Buffet—$9.95 per person—All you can eat!" Your mother stops the car. You and your brothers and sisters pile out. As the orange globe of the sun sets over the water, you enter the restaurant and enjoy the wonderful smells.

You pick up your plate at the beginning of the steam table and start down the line. But as you hungrily reach for the first item, your stomach does a somersault: spiny sea urchins, red octopus (their tentacles sticking to your hand as you pick them up), brown turban snails, starfish, innkeeper worms, and barnacles. Although this seafood buffet would not appeal to most people, it would be just what a sea otter ordered!

Study this "Sea Otter Menu," then play the "Seafood Buffet Game!"

Sea Otter Menu

Abalone

Barnacles

Brown Turban Snail

Chiton

Clam

Innkeeper Worm

Mussel

Purple Sea Urchin

Red Octopus

Red Sea Urchin

Rock Crab

Scallop

Sea Star

Seafood Buffet Game Directions

Ride on a kelp slide and dive into the ocean to find a "Seafood Buffet" to feed your otter!

The game includes:
- The game board
- Four cut-out sea otter playing pieces on page 21
- "Sea Otter Menu" on page 15

You need:
- Scissors
- Energy tokens: beans, pennies, paper clips, OR small pieces of paper (about 30)

Before playing:
- Cut out the sea otter playing pieces on page 21.
- Color them so they look very different.
- Fold along the solid lines so the pictures face outward.
- Overlap the flaps to form a base and tape or paste together.
- Study the "Sea Otter Menu."

Objective:
- Make wise choices so that your otter can be the first to make it to the finish with 15 energy tokens.

To play:
- Place your otters on the same side of the board.
- Place your energy tokens between the players. Up to four players can play.
- Decide who will go first.
- Take turns moving your otters. You may move one space in any direction. When you land on a food space, take one energy token (one bean, penny, or paper clip).
- Sometimes a space does not have a picture of food. Read the information and do what it tells you to do.
- Move ahead and collect as much food as you can. You must balance your need to get food with the amount of energy it takes to get it. Beware of spaces that take away your energy (lose one turn).
- Look for kelp slides that move you quickly to other areas of the board. If you land on a gray kelp slide space, move your otter to the gray space at the other end, and rest there until your next turn, when you can again move one space in any direction—including continuing to slide, if you wish!
- If you land on a space that is occupied by another player, you may take that player's energy token away. (Some otters do take food from one another.)
- The first player to collect 15 energy tokens and reach the finish wins!

BEAVER
lodges make great dens for river otters.

Seafood Buffet Game

START

FINISH

KELP SLIDE

KELP SLIDE

You weigh 60 lbs. (27 kg) and must eat about 12 lbs. (5 kg) of food a day to stay warm and keep moving. TAKE ANOTHER TURN.

A male otter takes your food. LOSE ONE TURN.

Oil spill! LOSE TWO TURNS.

You develop a method for grabbing sea birds to eat while you are underwater. EARN ONE ENERGY POINT.

You eat so many purple sea urchins that your teeth and bones are stained purple. EARN ONE ENERGY POINT.

You make 24 dives for one abalone. LOSE ONE TURN.

White shark attack. LOSE TWO TURNS.

You dig up the sandy bottom looking for clams. EARN ONE ENERGY POINT.

Sea urchins damage kelp beds. Eating sea urchins keeps kelp beds healthy. TAKE ANOTHER TURN

Conflict with abalone hunters. LOSE ONE TURN.

You must eat many snails to make a meal. LOSE ONE TURN.

KELP SLIDE

KELP SLIDE

Your teeth become old and worn. LOSE ONE TURN.

Storm at sea. You are separated from pup. LOSE ONE TURN.

Sea **17** OTTER

Sink or Swim

Imagine—living your whole life on the sea like the sea otter!

As you compare yourself to an otter, think about the special features that allow an otter to live in the sea.

How long could you hold your breath underwater?

The average person can hold his or her breath for a minute or less. An otter can hold its breath for four to five minutes. An otter's lungs are more than twice as large as the lungs of other marine mammals about the same size.

How deep could you dive?

Although sea otters generally dive in water that is 80–100 feet (24–30 m) deep, they have been known to dive to depths of more than 400 feet (122 m). "Breath-hold" divers (people who dive without scuba equipment) can go only to 30 or 40 feet (9–12 m) deep.

How well could you see underwater?

When you open your eyes underwater, objects look blurry. The only way you can see clearly underwater is by wearing goggles or a face mask. Otters can see clearly in both air and water. The structure of the otter's eyeball allows it to focus more clearly on objects underwater.

Even an otter cannot see well in murky water. Look at the otter's face on the cover of your book. What features might help an otter locate fish in cloudy water? Its whiskers! The otter's front paws are very sensitive and also aid the animal in locating food in murky conditions.

How long could you swim on your back? How long is your little toe? What does the length of your little toe have to do with living in the ocean? Read on!

Sea otters spend much of their time on their backs. Their toes help make this possible. Otter feet and people feet are opposite. Your outside toe is the shortest on your foot. An otter's outside toe is the longest on its back feet. What does this long, outside toe do for the shape of the otter's foot? The otter's foot is shaped like a flipper.

Otters can see clearly in both air and water.

Whiskers aid otters in murky water.

An otter's front paws are sensitive and nimble.

Otters store food items in loose folds of skin that are under each front leg.

An otter's lungs are more than twice as large as the lungs of other marine mammals.

Think of the last time you went swimming then answer the questions.

How long could you stay in the water before you became chilled?

Otters live in waters with temperatures between 35 and 60 degrees F (2–15°C). A human who accidentally falls into water that is 40 degrees F (4°C) could live for only a few minutes.

Otter fur is dense. One square inch of sea otter underfur has 600,000 to over 1,000,000 separate hairs. A human has about 100,000 hairs on his or her head. Otter fur is unique. It is made up of two layers: waterproofing guard hairs and thick underfur. The dense undercoat traps air bubbles that retain heat from the body and insulates the animal against the cold ocean waters.

Most marine mammals have thick layers of fat that insulate them from the cold. Sea otters do not. Because their fur protects them against the cold, they take care of it by frequent grooming.

Sea otters also hold their feet out of the water. How does this help to keep them warm? Their dark colored feet absorb heat from the sun. Their paws and feet have little fur. They keep them dry so they do not lose heat to the cold water.

When you are swimming or diving, how many shells or rocks can you carry to the surface in one trip?

Sea otters forage on the ocean bottom for their food and tools. Wouldn't it be handy if they had "pockets" to carry their materials to the surface? Otters are able to store food items in loose folds of skin that are under each of their front legs. They can even store several spiky sea urchins.

What feature allows the otter to pick things up (like shells) or to manipulate tools? The otter's front paws are sensitive and nimble. In murky water they reach into crevices and pat around surfaces to find food.

CRAYFISH
is a common food for river otters.

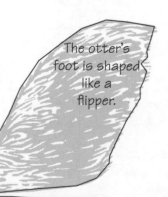

The otter's foot is shaped like a flipper.

Dark colored feet absorb heat from the sun.

Otter fur is made up of two layers: waterproofing guard hairs and thick underfur that insulates the animal.

Sink or Swim Puzzle Directions

Build a sea otter to learn about its special features for life in the sea!

The game includes:

- The otter diagram on pages 18 and 19
- The features (drawn within puzzle pieces) on the next page

You need:

- Crayons, markers, or color pencils
- Scissors
- Glue or paste

Before playing:

- Review the information in "Sink or Swim" that compares people and otters.

To play:

- Read the otter diagram on pages 18 and 19 for clues about what an otter needs to live in the sea. Then study the features drawn inside the puzzle pieces. Color the pieces that contain features a sea otter needs to survive in its sometimes harsh environment.
- When you have colored all necessary features for your otter to swim, cut out the pieces. If you can place the pieces into the diagram so they form a complete otter, then you have an otter that will swim! When you're sure they are in the correct positions, paste the pieces onto the diagram to finish the picture.

DENS
of river otters are
located in rocks or
hollow logs.

ENHYDRA LUTRIS
is the scientific
name of sea
otters.

Sink or Swim Puzzle Pieces

Fold here (to fit between pages 18 and 19)

Cut along dashed line to neatly remove page from book

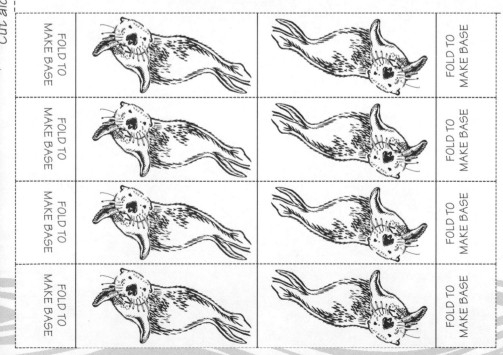

FOLD TO MAKE BASE

FOLD TO MAKE BASE

FOLD TO MAKE BASE

FOLD TO MAKE BASE

FOLD TO MAKE BASE

FOLD TO MAKE BASE

FOLD TO MAKE BASE

FOLD TO MAKE BASE

Seafood Buffet Otter Playing Pieces

Cut out these sea otters to play the "Seafood Buffet Game" on page 17.

Tools of the Trade

Have you ever gone "crabbing"? Would you catch a crab with your bare hands? Probably not!

When I was a little girl, I lived on the Indian River in Delaware and my mother used to take me crabbing. She showed me the tools and techniques for catching crabs.

We woke up early on crabbing day. The weather would be too hot if we waited until afternoon. We carried a bushel basket and a burlap bag, string, wood stakes, sinkers, bait, and nets to the riverbank. We tied the bait and sinkers to one end of the string and tossed it into the shallow water. We tied the other end of the string to a stake on the shore. And then we waited. Soon, one by one, the lines would move. The crabs gently jerked the lines as they fed on the bait.

Bent over, but careful to keep my shadow out of the water, I pulled in a line very slowly. It was hard to be patient. If I pulled the line too swiftly, the crab would let go of the bait. I began to think that crabs were smarter than people gave them credit.

Just as I lifted the crab from the muddy river bottom, *swish,* my mother scooped it into the net. With practice, I also snared the big blue crabs, their wet claws clicking in the sunlight. But I was never as skilled as my mother. After the crab was netted, we placed it in the basket with seaweed and a burlap sack over the top for shade. I remember feeling proud when our whole family enjoyed the steamed crabs that I had helped catch.

Through the ages, people have used tools to gather food and to do work. But scientists who study behavior have discovered that humans are not the only animals that use tools.

FROGS
are a favorite
food of river
otters.

Tools of the Trade Directions

To learn about other animals that use tools, play the "Tools of the Trade Game."

Sea otters use rocks as hammers to pound open the thick shells of mollusks, or as "crowbars" to pry sea urchins loose from crevices. A sea otter may place a flat rock on its stomach and smack a food item against it. Or the otter may use a second rock to hit the clam or mussel resting on the flat rock on its stomach.

Sea otters do not limit themselves to rocks. They also use shells, driftwood, and the **carapace** (the empty hard shell) of a crab as tools. They may even pound two food items (such as clams) against each other.

The game includes:
- "Tools of the Trade Animal Cards" on page 25
- "Tools of the Trade Tool Cards" on page 27

You need:
- Scissors
- A flat playing surface

Before playing:
- Cut out the Animal and Tool Cards.
- Place the cards in rows on a flat surface. You may want to place three cards in six rows. All the picture (animal or tool) sides of the cards should be face up.

Objective:
- To match the animal with the tool that it uses

To play:
- Decide who will go first. Match the animal with a tool that you think it might use.
- When you think you have a match, turn the cards over. If the text on the animal card is the same as the text on the tool card, you have a match. Pick up the two cards and place them in a pile in front of you.
- If the information does not match, turn the cards back over so that only the pictures show.
- When all the cards have been picked up, the player with the most correct matches wins.
- Check the answer key on page 64.

GROOMING
is critical for
cleaning the sea
otter's fur.

Tools of the Trade Animal Cards

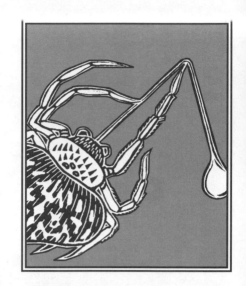
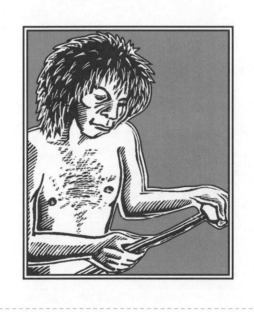

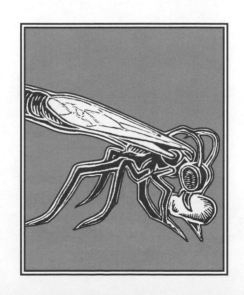

Bola Spider

The female spider makes a bola from silk. From her perch on a branch, she swings it back and forth to snag a moth that strays within her range.

Shrike

A shrike behaves like a hawk, but it does not have the powerful feet to either kill or hold its prey. After it kills an animal with its strong beak, it impales its meal on the thorns of bushes. With its prey secure, the shrike feeds on it.

Darwin Finch

The Darwin finch grasps a thorn in its beak and drills into the bark of a tree or stump, searching for insects that live under the bark. Using the thorn again, the finch spears an insect, pulls it out, shifts the tool to its feet, and then eats its meal.

Sea Otter

Individual sea otters seem to prefer different tools and even use them differently. Some will retain a favorite rock in the loose folds of skin located under each foreleg.

Chimpanzee

Chimpanzees use tools more than any other animal except humans. They use leaves for collecting water and for bandages. They push twigs into termite holes, remove the sticks, and then eat the termites that are clinging to them.

Human

Early people made tools from stone, bone, and wood. Through time, human tools have become more sophisticated. Today computers are a valuable tool for people involved in many different kinds of work.

Egyptian Vulture

Egyptian vultures open ostrich eggs by throwing rocks at them. The bird holds a stone in its beak, tips back its head and then snaps it forward, hurling the stone at the egg. The egg cracks after a few hard hits.

Solitary Wasp

The solitary wasp uses a pebble like a hammer. Grasping a pebble in its jaws, the wasp pounds the earth to close up its burrow. Sometimes it tamps down the dirt with just its head and jaws.

Archerfish

The archerfish has perfected the "liquid arrow." Spying a dragonfly resting on a leaf, the fish sucks in water, moves to the surface, aims, and shoots. The dragonfly is knocked into the pond and the fish feeds.

Tools of the Trade Tool Cards

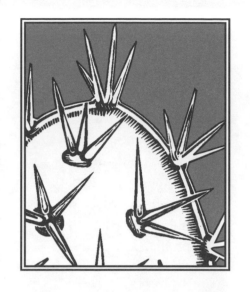

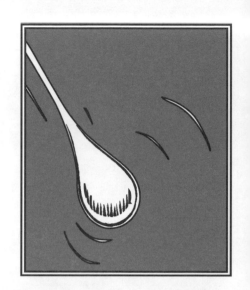

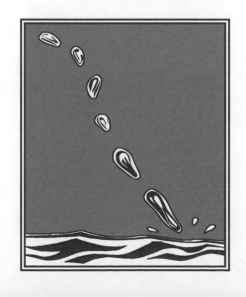

Bola

The female spider makes a bola from silk. From her perch on a branch, she swings it back and forth to snag a moth that strays within her range.

Thorn Bush

A shrike behaves like a hawk, but it does not have the powerful feet to either kill or hold its prey. After it kills an animal with its strong beak, it impales its meal on the thorns of bushes. With its prey secure, the shrike feeds on it.

Cactus Thorn

The Darwin finch grasps a thorn in its beak and drills into the bark of a tree or stump, searching for insects that live under the bark. Using the thorn again, the finch spears an insect, pulls it out, shifts the tool to its feet, and then eats its meal.

Rock, Bottle, or Crab Shell

Individual sea otters seem to prefer different tools and even use them differently. Some will retain a favorite rock in the loose folds of skin located under each foreleg.

Leaves and Twig

Chimpanzees use tools more than any other animal except humans. They use leaves for collecting water and for bandages. They push twigs into termite holes, remove the sticks, and then eat the termites that are clinging to them.

Stone Tools to Computers

Early people made tools from stone, bone, and wood. Through time, human tools have become more sophisticated. Today computers are a valuable tool for people involved in many different kinds of work.

Rock

Egyptian vultures open ostrich eggs by throwing rocks at them. The bird holds a stone in its beak, tips back its head and then snaps it forward, hurling the stone at the egg. The egg cracks after a few hard hits.

Pebble

The solitary wasp uses a pebble like a hammer. Grasping a pebble in its jaws, the wasp pounds the earth to close up its burrow. Sometimes it tamps down the dirt with just its head and jaws.

Stream of Water

The archerfish has perfected the "liquid arrow." Spying a dragonfly resting on a leaf, the fish sucks in water, moves to the surface, aims, and shoots. The dragonfly is knocked into the pond and the fish feeds.

Guide to Otters of the World

Otters live throughout the world. Australia and Antarctica are the only continents without otters. Otters live in rivers and streams, lakes, marshes, and coastal areas in North America, Central and South America, Europe, Asia, and Africa. The only areas they don't live in are deserts, the highest mountains, and the polar regions.

Of the thirteen species of otters, eight are considered threatened or endangered. Much otter habitat is also threatened, by population growth and development, and by pollution.

This guide will introduce you to the otters of the world. Use the maps to find where each otter lives. Examine the picture of each otter, carefully drawn to scale, to see the differences among the species. And read about the otter's diet, habitat, and status.

Find out about these otters and more in the "Guide to Otters of the World."

HABITAT
for river otters
needs to be
pollution-free.

Aonyx capensis

Cape Clawless River Otter

Location: Senegal to Ethiopia, south to South Africa

Diet: crabs, frogs, catfish, mudfish

Habitat: rain forest, open coastal plains, semiarid country. This animal prefers still ponds and slow streams. Although it is usually near water, it may wander over land.

Sign: piles of cracked shells of crabs, clams, and other mollusks

Status: To the three otters that are endemic to Africa (Aonyx capensis, Aonyx congicus, Lutra maculicollis), the greatest threat is the increasing human population. To feed more people, the land is changed to farmland and overgrazed by livestock. Although this animal is widespread throughout middle and southern Africa, it is not abundant anywhere.

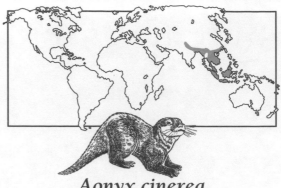

Aonyx cinerea

Asian Small-clawed River Otter

Location: northwestern India to southeastern China and Malay Peninsula, southern India, Hainan, Sumatra, Java, Borneo, Palawan

Diet: crabs, other crustaceans, mollusks, frogs, small fish

Habitat: streams, rice fields, mangrove forests

Status: This population is still widespread.

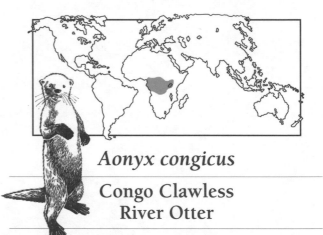

Aonyx congicus

Congo Clawless River Otter

Location: southeastern Nigeria and Gabon to Uganda and Burundi

Diet: small land vertebrates, eggs, frogs, worms, insects

Habitat: Scientists know little about this species. These animals seem to prefer mountain streams within rainforests. However, because of some of its physical characteristics (scanty hair, poorly developed whiskers, and its teeth) scientists think that this animal may live more on the land than other otters.

Status: This otter has declined due to excessive hunting.

I C E
River otters slide on ice and snow.

Enhydra lutris

Sea Otter

Location: originally found in coastal waters off Hokkaido, Sakhalin, Kamchatka, Commander Islands, Pribilof Islands, Aleutians, southern Alaska, British Columbia, Washington, Oregon, California, and western Baja California

Diet: purple sea urchins, octopus, abalone, brown turban snails, rock crabs, clams, mussels, scallops, barnacles, sea stars, chiton, innkeeper worms, other marine invertebrates, and slow-moving fish

Habitat: This animal may sometimes "haul out" on the land, but is able to live its entire life on the sea. This animal is rarely found more than half a mile (1 km) from the beach (juveniles sometimes stray farther).

Status: The population was listed as threatened in 1977 under the U.S. Endangered Species Act. Of all mammals, the pelt of the sea otter may be the most valuable. Beginning in 1741, sea otters were excessively hunted for their fur. By 1911 when a treaty was signed to protect these animals, only about 1,000 to 2,000 survived. Under protection, the sea otter has increased in numbers. The southern sea otter was once believed to be extinct. But a small group of about 30 animals survived and increased.

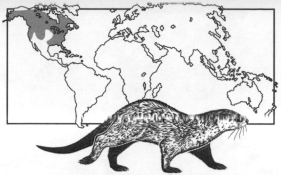

Lutra canadensis

North American River Otter

Location: Alaska, Canada, United States

Diet: fish, frogs, crayfish, turtles, aquatic beetles, clams, snails, snakes, salamanders, birds, freshwater crabs, plants

Habitat: coastal areas (salty and brackish waters); estuaries; freshwater lakes, streams, and rivers

Status: All species of river otters have been reduced by destruction of habitat, water pollution, pesticides, or excessive trapping for their furs. Otters have also been hunted because people thought the animals were competing with them for sport or commercial fish. Reintroduction programs have been successful in many areas throughout the river otter's former range.

JAW
River otters have strong jaws for eating fish.

Lutra felina
Marine Otter

Location: Pacific coast from northern Peru to Tierra del Fuego

Diet: fish, crustaceans, mollusks

Habitat: along the rocky shores of the Pacific Ocean

Status: These otters are endangered. They are often shot by commercial fishermen because they believe otters damage the supply of freshwater prawns. They are sometimes killed by fishing operations or are hunted for their skins.

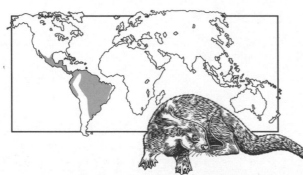

Lutra longicaudis
Neotropical River Otter

Location: northwestern Mexico to Uruguay

Diet: fish, crabs

Habitat: forest streams, lakes, swamps, marine coves

Status: This species is threatened by habitat destruction, water pollution, and illegal hunting. Population levels are low. It is classified as endangered under the U.S. Endangered Species Act.

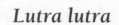

Lutra lutra
Eurasian River Otter

Location: western Europe to northeastern Siberia and Korea, Asia Minor, Himalaya region, southern India, China, Burma, Thailand, northwestern Africa, British Isles, Sri Lanka, Sakhalin, Japan, Taiwan, Sumatra, Java

Diet: fish, eels, crustaceans, birds, mammals, snakes

Habitat: freshwater and coastal habitats. These otters live in coastal areas only where rain is abundant, creating pools of fresh water for the animals to drink and bathe. Freshwater areas include rivers, lakes, and marshes. This animal is generally alone and active mainly at night.

Sign: rolling places (where animals "dry off" by rolling in the grass); slides; feeding sites (in winter ice holes are kept open); runways; and places where animals scratch, urinate, and defecate.

Status: This species has declined drastically in some areas. Some populations have been classified as endangered. These animals suffer from loss of habitat.

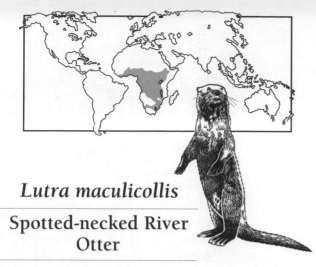

Lutra maculicollis

Spotted-necked River Otter

Location: Sierra Leone to Ethiopia to South Africa

Diet: fish, frogs, crayfish, crabs, rodents, rabbits

Habitat: inland waterways, estuaries, marine coves

Status: Although this animal is widely distributed, it is not abundant anywhere.

Lutra perspicillata

Smooth River Otter

Location: southern Iraq, Pakistan to Indochina and Malay Peninsula, Sumatra

Diet: fish

Habitat: large rivers, estuaries, mangrove swamps, freshwater wetlands

Status: This animal lives in small family groups. Of all the Asian otters, it is the most common throughout its range.

Lutra provocax

Southern River Otter

Location: Chile, western Argentina

Diet: crustaceans, clams

Habitat: rivers, lakes, estuaries, coastal areas. These animals prefer the cover of dense vegetation near the shoreline where they live.

Status: These otters are severely threatened. The population is very low. (The three otter species that live in South America—the giant otter, the marine otter, and the southern river otter—are severely threatened because forests are being destroyed and land is being drained and cleared for farming.)

KELP
beds are common resting areas of sea otters.

Lutra sumatrana

Hairy-nosed River Otter

Location: Indochina, Thailand, Malay Peninsula, Sumatra, Java, Borneo

Diet: fish, frogs, crayfish, crabs, rodents, rabbits

Habitat: inland waterways, estuaries, marine coves

Status: This species is the rarest of the Asian otters. It is almost extinct in the northern part of its range; its status is uncertain in other areas. Little is known about this species.

Pteronura brasiliensis

Giant Otter

Location: Columbia, Venezuela, Guiana, eastern Ecuador and Peru, Brazil, Bolivia, Paraguay, Uruguay, and northeastern Argentina

Diet: fish, crabs

Habitat: slow-flowing rivers and streams in forests, swamps, and marshes. It prefers streams where there is good cover and the bank slopes gently to the water.

Sign: Some otters create "campsites" on riverbanks. Giant otters make large campsites and use them for resting, feeding, and grooming. Campsites are easy to recognize because the otter digs up and tramples all the vegetation in a large area. These animals sometimes travel in large family groups of up to 20 animals.

Status: Giant otters are endangered. They are hunted for their valuable fur. The animal has disappeared over some parts of its range.

LUTRA CANADENSIS
is the scientific name
for North American
river otters.

MAMMALS
Sea otters are
related to skunks
and weasels.

Otters of the World Activity

Can you identify an otter by the signs it leaves in its habitat?

Examine these three pictures. Think about what you have just read in the "Otter Guide." Match the otter signs and habitat in each picture with information from the guide. Then write the name of the otter that left those signs on the line below the picture.

_____

_____

NATURE
Otters are an
essential part
of nature.

Just What an Otter Ordered

We know that some items on an otter's seafood buffet would not interest us, but what if a river and a sea otter compared "plates." A sea otter's "plate" might have abalone, sea urchins, rock crabs, red octopus, or brown turban snails—animals found in the sea. A river otter would relish fish of many kinds, frogs, crayfish, and turtles—creatures from freshwater habitats.

Take a close look at the skull and teeth of the river and the sea otter. Studying an animal's teeth can help us determine its diet.

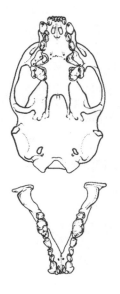

River otter teeth

The river otter has 36 teeth. (Adult humans have 32.) Teeth have different names and functions. **Incisors** have sharp, straight cutting edges. They are found at the front of the mouth and are used for biting. River otters have 12 incisors that are used for biting off small pieces of meat.

Canines (or dog teeth) look like a dog's fangs. River otters have four canines and use them for grasping fish and breaking through the tough skin on fish.

The river otter has 14 **premolars.** The front premolars shear the food as it is being chewed. The back premolars and six **molars** that are broad and flat grind up the shells of crayfish and crush bones.

OTTERS
both sea and
river, like to
play.

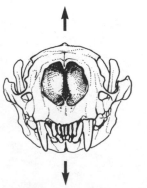

This diagram is the front view of the sea otter skull. The arrows demonstrate how the skull is opened up to show the view of the teeth for each of the skulls—river otter, sea otter, and human—in the illustrations on these two pages.

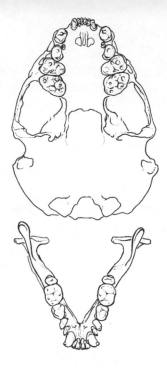

Sea otter teeth

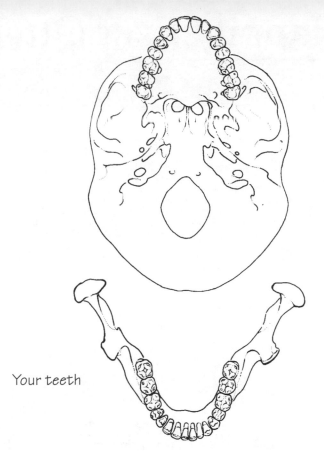

Your teeth

The sea otter's canine teeth are heavy and often blunt so that the animal can pry open shells. Once the shell is open, the sea otter removes the soft meat inside with its canines. Or the otter may use its flat, broad premolars and molars for crushing shells. The sea otter has specialized incisors on the lower jaw that are "spadelike." These teeth allow the sea otter to "clean its plate" by scraping the last of its prey from the shell.

Notice the difference in size between the river otter, sea otter, and human skulls. Compare sizes by looking at the **humerus** bone of the upper arm. Compare the shape of an otter's humerus bone to yours. The curve in the bone is unique to sea mammals, and shows that otters use their forearms for swimming.

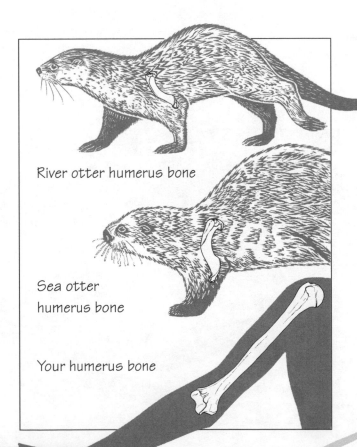

River otter humerus bone

Sea otter humerus bone

Your humerus bone

Happily Ever Otter

How many stories have you read that end "and they lived happily ever after"? Many North American otter reintroduction stories are having "happy endings"—that is, "new beginnings" for river otter populations.

River otters once lived throughout most of North America. Native Americans hunted otters and used their fur for clothing. However, when European settlers arrived, they threatened otter populations by cutting down forests and clearing land for farming. Rivers and streams where otters lived suffered when chemicals from pesticides and fertilizers seeped into the water.

By the 1980s eleven states no longer had otters. The animals were considered rare in thirteen others. The time had come to take action!

Jane Griess was a graduate student at the University of Tennessee when several biologists and state and federal agencies decided to take action in Great Smoky Mountains National Park.

Great Smoky Mountains National Park spreads across the states of Tennessee and North Carolina. Most of the rugged Great Smoky Mountains are contained within the park. The park has thick forests with over 130 different kinds of native trees and 733 miles (1,180 km) of clear, cold streams. In national parks wild animals are not hunted and are allowed to live as naturally as their ancestors did hundreds of years ago.

The environment and the conditions in the park were right for otters, but otters had not been seen in the area for almost fifty years! Jane Griess was a member of the team that reintroduced otters into Great Smoky Mountains National Park in 1986.

A young woman with a long blond braid and a friendly Tennessee accent, Jane had her hands full transporting and caring for fourteen river otters. The otters were trapped in North Carolina and shipped to Tennessee by plane and car. (Otters are very sensitive to stress. In fact, two otters transported by car died when the journey was disrupted by a snowstorm.) On February 14, 1986, Jane found herself in a small plane flying just ahead of a snowstorm with a number of caged otters protesting loudly.

Arriving at the park, the animals were not released immediately but were housed in a converted chicken house. What kind of houseguests were otters? According to Jane, they were picky eaters. Jane attempted to feed them a prepared diet of horse meat, bone and fish meal, vegetables, and vitamins. But the wild otters would settle for nothing less than fresh fish.

The otters had very different personalities, but Jane refrained from naming them. Researchers did not want to grow attached to these intriguing creatures whose pranks—even on a bad day—made them smile.

After one week the animals underwent surgery. Veterinarians placed small radio transmitters inside each animal. The otters were held for a few more days to ensure they had recovered and were then released in groups of two to three into a slow moving creek in Great Smoky Mountains National Park. Eleven otters were released.

After the otters were freed, Jane tracked their movements from the ground and from the air. Bumping along roads in an old truck, flying in a small plane with an antenna mounted on each wing, or most often, hiking the back country, often eight to ten miles (13–16 km) a day, Jane searched for the signals given off by transmitters inside each animal. In addition, Jane searched the areas where animals had been located for **scat**. The scat (or droppings) was analyzed to discover what otters ate.

PUPS
play as protective mothers watch over them.

Information about diet was critical. Why? Some **anglers** (people who fish for fun) were not happy about the National Park Service introducing otters into the famous trout waters of Great Smoky Mountains National Park. They feared that otters would eat too many trout and affect their sport.

Jane discovered that crayfish were the most common food eaten by the otters, followed by fish. Fish was an important food source because it was available year-round. But the fish prized by otters was not trout. Otters seemed to prefer the slower swimming fish. Why? They were easier to catch! Supported by other studies, Jane maintained that by removing fish that compete with trout for food, otters may actually help the sport fish.

Jane continued to track the otters for about thirteen months. She expected the batteries in the transmitters to last about that long.

Was this project a success? Jane concluded, yes! The reintroduction into Great Smoky Mountains National Park was a success compared to other successful otter programs. However, Jane knew that the true test was whether or not the otters mated and had young.

Growing up in Tennessee, did Jane always know she wanted to be a wildlife biologist? "No, I didn't always think about becoming a biologist, but I believe it was my mother who instilled in me an appreciation and love for wildlife. Mom was into feeding birds and taking my six brothers and sisters and me on nature hikes. Mom would always stop the car and move a turtle off of the road. Using an eye dropper and baby bottle, she helped me raise orphaned wild baby animals."

QUICK!
Steering with their
tails, otters speed
along underwater.

At age sixteen, Jane became familiar with the Great Smoky Mountains when she worked at a lodge. That summer she made beds, chopped wood, hiked the trails of the famous misty mountains, and answered questions from visitors, such as "How often does the sun rise around here?"

Jane graduated from the University of Tennessee in 1987 with a Master of Science degree after she completed her otter reintroduction work. Today she is a biologist with the United States Fish and Wildlife Service at the Rocky Mountain Arsenal, an urban wildlife refuge near Denver, Colorado.

In 1988, Jane received a phone call from a colleague. In the area in which she had originally released the eleven otters someone saw a large otter with three young ones. Not only had Jane's otters survived, but they had mated and produced young.

In the winter of 1992, ten more river otters were released into Great Smoky Mountains National Park. A total of thirty-seven otters have been released into the park since Jane began her work in 1986. Park wildlife biologist Kim DeLozier is planning more releases in the future.

Successful otter reintroduction stories also come from Colorado, Missouri, Ohio, Kentucky, and North Carolina. But the "happily ever afters" are not just for the river otters. Hiking, fishing, or daydreaming by a riverbank, people, too, will have the opportunity to watch these delightful creatures at home in their natural habitat.

THE *Happy* END!

Otter Moves

What do otters and submarines have in common? The shape of otters and submarines allows them to move more easily through water. If an otter were shaped like a box, it would have to work much harder and burn up more energy (therefore requiring more food) to overcome a physical force known as "drag." Otters have been practicing the laws of physics for thousands of years—long before humans even suspected the laws existed.

From the shape of its claws to the shape of its body, the otter is well suited for its wet lifestyle. The otter's body is shaped like a cylinder.

When an otter swims quickly underwater, it does everything to maintain its cylindrical shape. The front feet are flattened against the body. The hind feet are held alongside the tail. This position streamlines the animal and allows it to slip more quickly through the water.

In this position the otter uses its feet only for maneuvering. The otter's speed comes from an up-and-down motion, a "flexing" of its entire body. This movement begins at the head and neck, progresses through the shoulders and the rest of the body, and moves right through to the very tip of the tail.

The next time you are in a swimming pool, try to copy this movement. Put your legs together and your arms at your sides. Try to propel yourself with an undulating, or wave-like, action. You will have an easier time imitating this motion with the swimming otter you can build on this page.

The otter also uses its short, powerful legs to propel itself underwater. The animal strokes and glides. The webbed feet add to the power of the otter's stroke. When swimming slowly underwater or on the surface, the river otter, using all four legs, doggy-paddles.

X

X

S2

Build swimming otter here

X

X

S3

The otter's tail works in many ways. When the otter is swimming underwater the tail acts like a "rudder" and helps steer the animal. On land when the otter stands on its back feet—usually for a better view of things—the tail helps prop it up.

The otter's short legs suggest that the animal is not meant for extended overland travel. The otter actually runs more comfortably on land than it walks. When comparing the otter to land animals such as deer, coyotes, or wolves, the otter is rated slow. But an otter can run faster than a person.

An otter moves on land with a "humpbacked" gait, like a caterpillar. With its back arched and its tail stiff, the "otter walk" appears awkward. An otter run is a little smoother, but still does not qualify as graceful. As the hind feet move forward in a run, the otter rounds or arches its back. The otter straightens its back as the front feet reach out for the animal to jump ahead. See if you can imitate this movement with the walking otter you can build on this page.

When moving about on snow and ice, otters slide as often as they can. They jump a few steps and then glide! They often slide with their front feet at their sides and their back feet trailing. They also belly-slide down hills, sometimes sticking out their front feet to steer or brake on a fast hill. One otter was even observed sliding down a hill on its side! It used its front paw close to the ground to push.

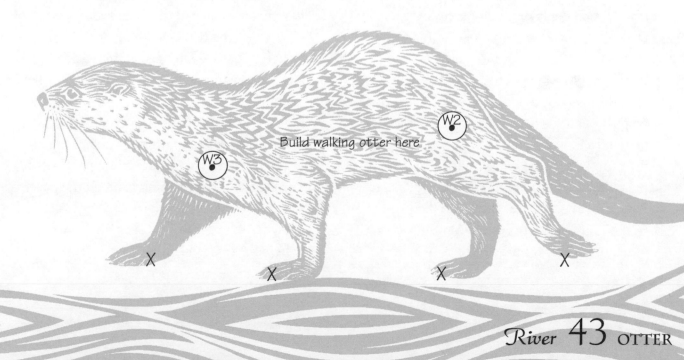

Build walking otter here

Otter Moves Directions

Make moving illustrations that show a river otter's swimming and walking motions.

Otters fascinate us for many reasons. Beyond their cute faces and winsome, playful ways, we cannot help but admire how well they "fit" their lifestyle. From head to tail, otters are well adapted for their way of life.

Objective:
- To cut out and assemble the otter models to imitate otter movements

The activity includes:
- The "Otter Moves" backgrounds on pages 42 and 43
- The "Otter Moves Model Parts" on page 45

You need:
- Scissors
- A pencil (it will help you poke holes more easily for the brads)
- Six 3/4–inch brads (also called paper fasteners)
- Paste or glue

Swimming Otter Assembly Directions
1. Cut out the pieces. Match the S1 circles, placing the control stick on the bottom, the head section in between, and the tail section on top. Poke a brad through the circles and fasten all three pieces together.
2. Place the S2 circle of the hind legs over the S2 circle of the tail section. Poke a brad through. (You will later fasten this to page 42.)
3. Place the S3 circle of the front legs over the S3 circle of the head section. Poke a brad through. (You will later fasten this to page 42.)
4. Place your swimming otter on page 42. Fasten the otter's hind legs to the page by poking the brad through the S2 circle on the page. Fasten the otter's front legs to the page by poking the brad through the S3 circle on the page. Do not poke the middle (S1) brad through the page.
5. Paste only the feet over the Xs on the page.
6. Gently pull the control stick from side to side to see how the otter moves when swimming.

Walking Otter Assembly Directions
1. Cut out the pieces. Match the W1 circles, placing the control stick on the bottom, the head section in between, and the tail section on top. Poke a brad through the circles and fasten all three pieces together.
2. Place the W2 circle of the back legs over the W2 circle of the tail section. Poke a brad through. (You will later fasten this to page 43.)
3. Place the W3 circle of the front legs over the W3 circle of the head section. Poke a brad through. (You will later fasten this to page 43.)
4. Place your swimming otter on page 43. Fasten the otter's back legs to the page by poking the brad through the W2 circle on the page. Fasten the otter's front legs to the page by poking the brad through the W3 circle on the page. Do not poke the middle (W1) brad through the page.
5. Paste only the feet over the Xs on the page.
6. Gently pull the control stick up and down to see how the otter moves when walking.

Otter Moves Model Parts

Swimming otter hind legs

Swimming Otter Model Parts

Swimming otter front legs

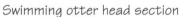

Swimming otter head section

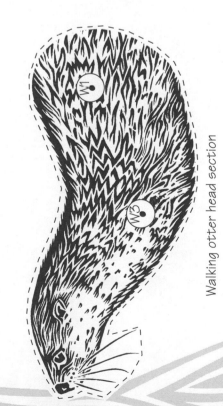

Swimming otter tail section

Swimming otter control stick

Walking Otter Model Parts

Walking otter back legs

Walking otter front legs

Walking otter tail section

Walking otter head section

Walking otter control stick

Cut along dashed line to neatly remove page from book

River 45 OTTER

Tiddly Frogs

River otters live in many different "wet places." Some live in the salt- and brackish water along the coasts. Others make their homes in high, cold mountain lakes. They seem to prefer streams, rivers, and estuaries. But one thing is common to all otter habitats: water.

Otters share their wet environments with many other animals: raccoons, beavers, muskrats, and moose! Bobcats, foxes, and coyotes often visit the waterways of otters.

Many birds share the otter's water address: loons, pelicans, cormorants, herons, egrets, ducks, geese, ospreys, and even bald eagles. Frogs and salamanders, turtles and snakes, and many different insects are not only "neighbors," but also are food for river otters.

River otters do not usually build their own dens. They either take over the den of another animal or use natural shelters. Otters sometimes take over abandoned beaver dens, or use hollow logs, piles of loose rock, logjams, or empty duck blinds. Sometimes they will build nests from vegetation.

The best time to see otters is from dawn to about ten in the morning and during the evening. They are generally busy feeding during these times. But even if you get up at 6:00 A.M., you may not see a river otter. River otters are shy around people.

However, you may see what the otter has left behind. Look for areas where the grass is matted down—an otter's rolling area. Search for tracks, dens, slides, feeding places, or **sprainting sites** (where animals defecate), haul-outs (where animals come out of the water), and runways (paths through the grass, sometimes between bodies of water). Slides may be found on riverbanks or in snow, even on flat ground as much as 25 feet (8 m) long. The scat of the otter has fish or crayfish parts in it. When fresh it is green and slimy.

Otters also leave "scent stations." They leave their scent on any raised area—a clump of dirt, a bush, or stone. Scent stations are common around dens, where otters roll in the grass to dry off, and near slides and runways.

RAFTS
of female sea otters rest in kelp beds.

Tiddly Frogs Game Directions

In the game "Tiddly Frogs," you get to be otter food!

Study the board on the following pages showing the otter's habitat. On the back of the game board, on page 52, you will find the Tiddly Frog Pond Field Guide to help you find otter signs. Note the different animals that share the otter's home.

The game includes:
- Directions for folding three origami frogs on page 49
- The playing board on pages 50 and 51

You need:
- Three 3-inch by 5-inch index cards for each player

Before playing:
- Fold three frogs for each player as shown on page 49.
- Carefully remove the game board from the book by cutting along the dashed lines. Tape the board together with the tape on the back.
- Place the game board on a hard, flat surface, such as a table or the floor.

Objective:
- To move your three frogs into the cattails in Tiddly Frog Pond and avoid becoming food for otters

To play:
- Decide who will go first.
- The first player puts one of his or her three frogs on the launching pad.
- The player pushes down on the back edge of the frog and causes it to leap.
- If the frog lands on any part of an otter, it is eaten and removed from the game.
- If the frog lands on the board, but not on an otter, it remains there and is flipped from that position during the player's next turn.
- If the frog leaps off the board, it is returned to start and the next player takes his or her turn.
- If the frog leaps all the way into the cattails in Tiddly Frog Pond, it is safe and the player scores a point.
- Frogs can continue to be played until (1) they are eaten, or (2) they make it into the cattails in Tiddly Frog Pond safely.
- When all frogs have been played, the game is over and the player who moved the most frogs into the cattails in Tiddly Frog Pond wins!

After playing:
- Color the game board. It will make a nice poster for your bedroom wall.

Tiddly Frogs Origami

Can you change a house into a frog?! Follow the easy directions below!

Step 1: Make a House

1A Fold a 3-inch by 5-inch card in half by bringing the long sides together. Unfold.

1B Fold the upper left corner down to meet the right long side making a triangle flap. Unfold.

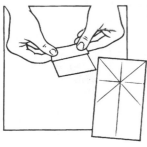

1C Fold the upper right corner down to meet the left long side making a triangle flap. Unfold.

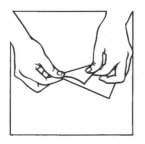

1D Flip over. Fold the top down making a crease through the middle of the "X" made by the other folds. Unfold.

1E Flip back over. Push in the sides where the horizontal crease goes through the "X" until the sides meet. Push the top down so it looks like a house.

Step 2: Change a House into a Frog

2A Fold the loose points of each of the little flaps on the roof of the house in half upward to meet at the top point of the roof.

2B Fold both sides below the roof in half inward, like closing doors, to meet at the center crease line.

2C Fold each of the little flaps on top in half downward and outward—like wings. But these are actually your frog's front legs!

2D Softly fold the bottom up to meet the top point. Don't make too hard of a crease. Then softly fold in half downward to meet the fold you just made.

2E Your finished frog should look like this! Tickle its back to make it jump!

LAUNCHING PAD

Tiddly Frog Pond Field Guide

Otter signs

A. Otter slide
B. Otter den
C. Hauling-out spot
D. Otter tracks

Other animals sharing otter habitat

1. Northern Harrier hawk
2. Moose
3. Beaver (den)
4. Swallowtail butterfly
5. Redwing blackbird
6. Cottontail rabbit
7. Pintail duck
8. River otters
9. Carp
10. Dragonfly
11. Painted turtle
12. Leopard frogs

Otter Editor

Have you ever read newspapers or magazines or known people who exaggerated the truth in order to tell a "good story"? Although these tales are exciting for the reader or listener, the misinformation in the story can hurt the reputation of the subject. Misinformation can change people's attitudes, causing them to fear or even dislike the subject.

What are some examples? Throughout history, snakes have been the victims of misinformation. People once said that snakes could hypnotize humans. They also said that rattlesnakes could spit venom for great distances. Obviously if you believed these stories, you would be afraid of snakes and would probably kill them every chance you had.

You need to be a good editor whenever you read or listen. What does an editor do? A good editor makes sure that writers (or speakers) have facts to back up what they are saying and then checks the facts to see if they are true. Editors also make sure that the conclusions drawn from the facts make sense.

The OTTER UPDATE

FREE

Vol. 1, No. 1

32 SEA OTTERS!
Discovered in an isolated cove – believed extinct!

SCIENTISTS REPORT AMAZING DISCOVERY

CALIFORNIA— Although biologists believed them to be extinct, a group of about 32 California sea otters were recently discovered thriving in a secluded cove.

Kept under wraps for 23 years, this isolated group was recently discovered by residents of the central Monterey County coast when the area was opened to motor traffic.

Biologists believe that the herd must have slowly increased from survivors from the early 1900s that were spared during this period of intense unrestricted hunting.

For more information see story on page 2…

Otter Editor Headlines

Be a good "otter editor" and decide which headlines are true and which are false.

Shown on the previous page and listed below are six newspaper headlines about otters. Be a good "otter editor" and decide which ones are true and which are false. If you have a red pencil or crayon, use that to mark out the false statements. Some newspapers have more than one headline, so be sure to read and check them all!

For explanations of all headlines (true or false) turn to page 2 of the newspaper (that is, the next page in your book).

STARFISH
are tasty treats
for hungry sea
otters.

The TABLOID TIMES

No Charge

Vol. 1, No. 1

GIGANTIC SERPENT SIGHTED IN POND!

Family fishing flees in terror...

EXCLUSIVE PHOTOS

Eyewitness's shocking report:

"It was over thirty feet long!"

See "Serpent sighted," page 2

NEWS FROM OTTERS AROUND THE WORLD

European otters are | This morning reports | In rivers and streams in
from Brazil about the | the United States, river

THE IRRATIONAL INQUIRER

Vol. 1, No. 1

Priceless

EXTRA!

500 POUND OTTER EXPLODES!

Gorges on last fish in preparation for hibernation.
See "Otter explodes," page 2...

Exclusive!

Otter gluttons eat last trout in the United States...

Anglers are in a tangle over it!

See "Otter gluttons," page 2...

BELIEVE IT OR NOT!

TRUE LIFE TESTIMONIAL

Tracking otters an uplifting experience

...says biologist

See "Tracking otters," page 2...

ALL THE NATURE
NEWS
THAT'S FIT TO PRINT

Volume 1, Number 1

SPECIAL EDITION

FREE

BIGHORN FOR OTTERS SWAP!

Rumors are true...swaps are a good deal for all!

See "Otter swap," page 2

IN OTHER NEWS

The Denver Museum of Natural History announces the newest title in The Wonder Series: **Sea Otter River Otter**

Otter Editor Page 2

*Get the **true** stories behind the headlines!*

"Otters discovered,"
continued from page 1

TRUE: In the story "Otter Hunt," this group of otters was the one Tobias observed during the time he was stranded. The author likes to think Tobias's choice was to keep the otters' location a secret and protect them from being hunted. What was your choice for Tobias?

"Serpent sighted,"
continued from page 1

TRUE: Believe it or not, families of otters swimming in a line have been mistaken for "pond monsters." Playing something that looks like "follow the leader," these animals have appeared to be pond serpents 30 to 40 feet (9–12 m) long to people with very active imaginations!

FALSE: We really don't know anything about a family fleeing in terror—we made that up!

"Otter swap,"
continued from page 1

TRUE: Biologist Tom Beck proposed that Colorado trade its Rocky Mountain bighorn sheep for some of Oregon's river otters. That was six years ago. Today some twenty-four otters from Oregon live along a river in southwestern Colorado, and they seem to be doing pretty well. The river otter is an endangered species in Colorado. Some people thought Colorado was getting "ripped off" by exchanging a big animal for such a small one. As it turned out it was much easier for Colorado to fill its order than for Oregon to obtain and transport the otters.

This item appeared in the Rocky Mountain News, in Denver, Colorado. The reporter was Gary Gerhardt.

TOOLS
used by sea otters
include rocks, shells,
and driftwood.

"Otter explodes,"

continued from page 1

FALSE: River otters do not weigh 500 pounds. Males are generally larger than females; otters weigh from about 11 to 30 pounds (5–14 kg) and measure 35 to 52 inches (9–13 cm).

Although people once believed that otters hibernated, biologists have observed that they do not. Otters remain active in winter—even hunting under the ice of frozen ponds for fish.

"Otter gluttons,"

continued from page 1

FALSE: Otters have been accused of wiping out the fish that anglers like to catch. Although otters will occasionally take a trout or bass, they generally prefer the slower, bottom fish that are easier to catch. Trappers have also blamed otters for eating muskrats, mink, beaver, and other fur-bearing animals. Studies of otters' food habits show that otters rarely take any of these animals.

URCHINS
that sometimes
destroy kelp beds
are eaten by sea
otters.

"Tracking otters,"

continued from page 1

TRUE: Before biologist Jane Griess released ten river otters in Great Smoky Mountains National Park, the otters were implanted with radio transmitters. As the study progressed and the otters moved throughout the area, Jane tracked them from an airplane. When she located an otter, she could hear the steady rhythm of beeps in her headphones. This program was created to restore otters to east Tennessee where they have not lived since the early 1900s. They were wiped out because forests had been cut (their habitat destroyed) and they were trapped. You can read more about Jane and her study in the story titled "Happily Ever Otter."

A-Mazing Otters

Follow the maze and be an otter expert!

Well adapted to their individual lifestyles, river and sea otters are equally fascinating and wonderful animals. Although their environments can be quite different, they share certain qualities and habits. This maze will help you sort out their similarities and differences.

The game includes:
- The maze on pages 60 and 61
- The answer key on the last page

You need:
- Two pencils or crayons (different colors)

Before playing:
- Read the clues at right to review some of the things you have learned about otters in this book.

Objective:
- By following clues that suggest one or both species, you will take a path that leads you either to the river or sea otter.

To play:
- Begin at start. Decide if you will follow the sea otter or river otter path first.
- If you selected the river otter, as you move through the maze, stay on the path that contains clues that relate to river otters. Don't take any shortcuts or you may miss some clues!
- If you follow the clues correctly, you will come out of the maze at the river otter.
- After you have found the river otter, go back to start. With a different color pencil or crayon, follow all the clues that lead to the sea otter.

VERTICAL
Otters can stand
on their hind legs,
using their tails
for balance.

WHISKERS
help sea otters
find their way in
muddy water.

Sea Otter Clues

- Member of the weasel family, Mustelidae
- Lives in salt water
- Hind feet are large and flipper-like
- Tail is flattened and somewhat paddle-like
- Usually swims belly-up
- Females rest in groups called "rafts"
- Forages alone
- Sometimes at odds with anglers
- Helps kelp forests
- Curious, playful, opportunistic, social
- Young have to be taught to dive and forage
- Uses tools
- Eats abalone, sea urchins, crabs, mussels, and fish
- Threatened by pollution
- Sensitive front paws
- Eats, sleeps, mates, sometimes gives birth at sea
- Nearly extinct by the early 1900s

River Otter Clues

- Member of the weasel family, Mustelidae
- Lives mainly in fresh water, sometimes in salt water
- Will travel several miles over land
- Swims belly-down
- Humpbacked gait on land
- Occasionally preyed upon by wolves, eagles, and wolverines
- May hunt cooperatively
- Eats fish, turtles, frogs, crayfish, snakes, and birds
- Young don't instinctively know how to swim
- Threatened by pollution
- Sensitive front paws
- Can have up to four young in a litter
- Reintroduced in Great Smoky Mountains National Park, Tennessee, Colorado, and other states
- Plays on mud and snow slides
- Curious, playful, opportunistic, social
- Digs den in riverbanks
- Sometimes at odds with anglers

eXtinct
California sea otters were nearly extinct in the early 1900s.

A-Mazing Otters

TO RIVER OTTER

START

TO SEA OTTER

Lives mainly in fresh water, sometimes in salt water

Member of the weasel family, Mustelidae

Will travel several miles over land

Swims belly-down

Lives in salt water

Hind feet are large and flipper-like

Usually swims belly-up

Tail is flattened and somewhat paddle-like

Females rest in groups called "rafts"

Forages alone

RIVER OTTER

Sometimes at odds with anglers

Helps kelp forests

Digs den in riverbanks

Occasionally preyed upon by wolves, eagles, and wolverines

May hunt cooperatively

Eats fish, turtles, frogs, crayfish, snakes, and birds

Humpbacked gait on land

SEA OTTER

Young don't instinctively know how to swim

Nearly extinct by the early 1900s

Eats, sleeps, mates, sometimes gives birth at sea

Threatened by pollution

Sensitive front paws

Can have up to four young in a litter

Eats abalone, sea urchins, crabs, mussels, and fish

Young have to be taught to dive and forage

Uses tools

Reintroduced in Great Smoky Mountains National Park, Tennessee, Colorado, and other states

Curious, playful, opportunistic, social

Plays on mud and snow slides

Glossary

angler (AHN-glur)—person who fishes for fun or sport, in contrast to an individual who fishes for a living

bola (BOH-luh)—used by cowboys in South America for catching game or cattle. A rope shaped like the letter "Y." Weights are attached to the "arms" of the "Y." The rider holds the bola at the free end (the single end without weights), whirls it above his or her head, and then releases it.

brackish (BRAK-ish)—a mix of fresh and salt water

breath-hold diver (BREHTH-hohld DEYE-vuhr)—an individual who dives without equipment

crayfish (KRAY-fish)—a crustacean that lives in fresh water; related to and looks like a small lobster; an important food source for some river otters

crustacean (kruhs-TAY-shuhn)—an invertebrate (having no backbone) animal that has many jointed legs. This type of animal has no bones, but instead has a shell. Examples include lobsters, crabs, shrimp, and barnacles.

endangered (ihn-DAYN-juhrd)—animals that are threatened with extinction

endemic (ehn-DEHM-ihk)—species of plants or animals that have always lived in a particular place

estuary (EHSH-chuh-wehr-ee)—areas where fresh water and saltwater mix. Estuaries are very important because they are nurseries (where the young are born and raised) for many species.

extinct (ik-STIHNKT)—no longer living. Dinosaurs are extinct.

habitat (HAB-ih-tat)—the place where an animal lives, an animal's home

humerus (HYOOM-uh-rehs)—the long bone of the upper arm or forelimb that extends from the shoulder to the elbow.

intertidal (ihnt-uhr-TEYED-ehl)—the strip of the shoreline between the extremes of high and low tides

kayak (KEYE-ak)—a boat that looks like a canoe but with an enclosed deck. Kayaks have been used for thousands of years. Early people stretched animal hides over wooden frames. Today kayaks are made of fiberglass or a type of tough rubber.

kelp (KEHLP)—large brown seaweeds that grow in cold waters. Kelp forests that grow close to shore calm the waters and provide important habitat for many marine animals (such as sea otters, fish, and lobsters). Sea urchins and snails feed on kelp.

marine (muh-REEN)—of the sea

mollusk (MAHL-uhsk)—an animal with a soft body and no bones. Most mollusks have hard shells that protect their soft bodies. However, some have a special shell that is formed inside their bodies. An octopus is a mollusk and it has no shell at all.

origami (awr-uh-GAHM-ee)—the Japanese art of paper-folding

pelt (PEHLT)—the skin or hide of an animal

physics (FIHZ-ihks)—the science that explores ideas such as matter, energy, force, and time

protozoans (proht-uh-ZOH-uhnz)—single-celled, generally microscopic organisms

raft—a group of sea otters

scat (SKAT)—fecal matter or droppings of mammals

shrouds (SHROWDZ)—one of a set of ropes that stretches from the top of the ship's mast to the ship's sides

tentacle (TEHNT-ih-kuhl)—the arm of an octopus. An octopus has eight arms that it uses to catch crabs, lobsters, and clams.

threatened (THREHT-ehnd)—although the species may be abundant in some parts of the world, overall the population is being reduced.

YOUNG
*of sea otters may
be born on land or
in the sea.*

Bibliography

Barbeau, Marius. *Pathfinders in the North Pacific*. Caldwell, Idaho: The Caxton Printers, Ltd., 1958.

Bolin, R.L. "Reappearance of the southern sea otter along the California coast." *Journal of Mammalogy* 19(3):301-303, 1938.

Bolus, Malvina, editor. *People and Pelts: Selected Papers of the North American Fur Trade Conference*. Manitoba: Peguis Publishers, 1972.

Chanin, Paul. *The Natural History of Otters*. New York: Facts on File Publications, 1985.

Chapman, Joseph A., and George A. Feldhamer. *Wild Mammals of North America*. Baltimore: Johns Hopkins University Press, 1982.

Earley, Lawrence S. "On the rebound." *National Parks* 66(5-6): 34-38, 1992.

Foster-Turley, Pat, Sheila Macdonald, and Chris Mason, editors. *Otters: An Action Plan for their Conservation*. Gland, Switzerland: IUCN–The World Conservation Union, 1990.

George, Jean Craighead. *Beastly Inventions*. New York: David McKay Company, Inc., 1970.

Griess, Jane M. *River Otter Reintroduction in Great Smoky Mountains National Park*. Master's Thesis, Knoxville: University of Tennessee, 1987.

Grosvenor, Gilbert M. *The Marvels of Animal Behavior*. San Luis Obispo, California: Blake Publishing, 1972.

Murray, John A. *Wildlife in Peril: The Endangered Mammals of Colorado*. Niwot, Colorado: Roberts Rinehart Publishers, 1987.

Norwak, Ronald M. *Mammals of the World, Vol. II*. Baltimore: Johns Hopkins University Press, 1983.

Palmer, L.W. "The otter slaughter." *Oceans* 4(6):28-33, 1971.

Park, Ed. *The World of the Otter*. Philadelphia: J.B. Lippincott Company, 1971.

Riedman, Marianne. *Sea Otters*. Monterey, California: Monterey Bay Aquarium, 1990.

The River Otter Journal. 1(1), 1991.

Seton, Ernest Thompson. *Lives of Game Animals*. Boston: Charles T. Branford Co., 1953.

Streubel, Donald. *Small Mammals of the Yellowstone Ecosystem*. Niwot, Colorado: Roberts Rinehart Publishers, 1989.

Tumlison, Renn, and Scott Shalaway. *An Annotated Bibliography on the North American River Otter*. Oklahoma Cooperative Fish and Wildlife Research Unit and the Department of Zoology, Oklahoma State University, 1985.

Whitaker, John O. *The Audubon Society Field Guide to North American Mammals*. New York: Alfred A. Knopf, 1991.

Whitfield, Dr. Phillip. *The Hunters*. New York: Simon and Schuster, 1978.

Woolfenden, John. *The California Sea Otter: Saved or Doomed?* Pacific Grove, California: The Boxwood Press, 1985.

Answer Key

Sink or Swim Puzzle

Otters of the World

Giant Otter (*Pteronura brasiliensis*) "camp site" on river bank.

Cape Clawless River Otter (*Aonyx capensis*) leaves piles of cracked crab shells, clams, and other mollusks.

Eurasian River Otter (*Lutra lutra*) rolling place and pathway.

A-Mazing Otters

Acknowledgments

The Denver Museum of Natural History appreciates the encouragement, time, and support of the following individuals and organizations:

Project Sponsor — Valerie Gates

Publication Coordinator — Betsy R. Armstrong

Technical Review — Ellen Faurot-Daniels, Science and Education Director, Friends of the Sea Otter; Kim DeLozier, biologist, Great Smoky Mountains National Park; Dr. Steven K. Webster, Director of Education, and Nora Deans, Publications Editor, Monterey Bay Aquarium.

The Museum's Technical and Educational Team — Dr. Elaine Anderson, Diana Lee Crew, Joyce Herold, Dr. Cheri Jones, Karen Nein, Leslie Newell, and Peggy Zemach

Design — Gail Kohler Opsahl

Cover Illustration — Gail Kohler Opsahl

Illustration — Gail Kohler Opsahl and Marjorie C. Leggitt

Maps — Anthony G. Sanchez

We thank Alice Gray and Michael Shall and The Friends of The Origami Center of America, New York, New York, for allowing us to adapt their jumping frog origami.

Thanks to the kids who tested the activities: Mrs. Rogers' and Mrs. Sampson's students from North Middle School in Aurora, Colorado; and Alana Berland; Lynn Holmes; Rachel and Rebecca Lewis; Matt, Moe, and Molly McConaty; Elizabeth Mayne; Deena and Charlie Miller; Michael Murray; Rosie O'Dea; Erik Robbins; Jonathan and David Siegel; Kate Sneed; Chad Spurway; and Paige and Hokie Stapp.

For more information on sea otters, write to Friends of the Sea Otter, P.O. Box 221220 Carmel, CA 93922.